THE MOONBIRDS

THE M… ONBIRD

MARCH… D

by Mike Higgs

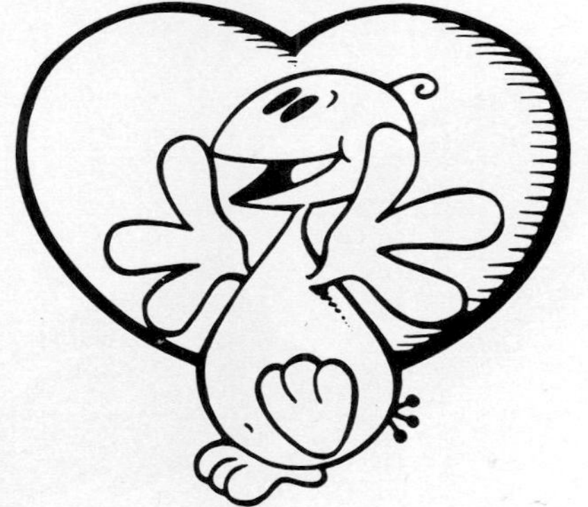

A Piccolo Original

Piccolo Books

The moonbirds live up on the moon. The leader of all the moonbirds is a giant creature called the Great Moonhawk. Only one Great Moonhawk is born about every one hundred years.

It was a special day on the moon because it was time for the Great Moonhawk's birthday.

No-one knew exactly how old the Great Moonhawk was but they knew that on this very day many years ago, he had hatched out of a golden egg.

Like all the Great Moonhawks before him, he had quickly grown to giant size and had then taken his place as ruler of the moonbird flock.

He had been a wise and kindly ruler and all the moonbirds wanted to make sure that he would have a nice time on his birthday.

They thought it would be a good idea to have some music at his birthday party, so all the moonbirds who could play a musical instrument were called together.

They formed themselves into a marching band and they made the most musical moonbird the leader. His name was Ludwig.

The Great Moonhawk's birthday party would be starting soon so all the musicians began to practice. They had a very strange collection of instruments.

One moonbird was trying to blow a huge brass horn called an Oom-pah-pah.

He couldn't get a single note out of it.

He got redder and redder in the face as he blew harder and harder.

The moonbird trying to play the Oom-pah-pah gave one last blow as hard as he possibly could. Something shot out of the end of the horn.

It was a tiny moonchick!

He had climbed into the horn, curled up and gone to sleep.

No wonder the moonbird couldn't get a note out of the horn.

Finally the band were ready to start playing and Ludwig started conducting them.

It sounded awful.

None of them had played together before and it was obvious that they would need a lot more practice before they were good enough to perform for the Great Moonhawk.

It was almost time for the Great Moonhawk's official birthday party to start but things were not getting any better. The sliding horn player kept hitting the fiddler in the back of the head and the fiddler almost poked the pipe player in the eye.

"This isn't working out very well at all," thought Ludwig. "We shall spoil the birthday party."

Ludwig was just wondering what else could go wrong when the ground began to shake. It was a moonquake.

The entire band fell down cracks that suddenly appeared in the ground.

Normally moonbirds fly into the air when a moonquake starts but the band had been so busy that they hadn't noticed it until it was too late.

The quake only lasted for a few seconds and after the dust had settled they all climbed up out of the cracks.

None of the moonbirds were hurt. They had just been shaken up.

Unfortunately, the same could not be said for their instruments.

All the pipes, trumpets, string instruments, drums and even the Oom-pah-pah were badly dented, twisted or broken.

"That does it," wailed Ludwig. "We definitely won't be able to play at the Great Moonhawk's birthday party now! Everything is ruined."

An old moonbird stepped up and said he had an idea. He told them that he had something at home that may just save the day.

The battered and dusty moonbird marching band all felt miserable as they followed the old moonbird to his home.

He produced a strange looking object. "I got this on one of my visits to earth," he said. "It's an old wind-up record player."

A record! That would provide the music they needed. Everyone felt much better.

The Great Moonhawk's birthday party started with a march-past by the newly formed Magnificent Moonbird Marching Band.

They all trooped past him with their battered instruments and pretended to play them while Ludwig carried the wind-up record player in front.

Everyone hoped that the Great Moonhawk would not notice that they were only miming to the record.

Of course, there isn't much that the Great Moonhawk doesn't notice but he did not say anything and applauded the band for giving a fine performance.

The party went very well and everyone enjoyed themselves.

The Great Moonhawk was very pleased that everyone liked him so much and would go to so much trouble to make his birthday a happy one.

mike higgs

MUSICAL MIX-UP

The Magnificient Moonbird Marching Band have got all their musical instruments into a terrible jumble. Can you sort them out and see how many instruments there are? See ANSWER panel for solution.

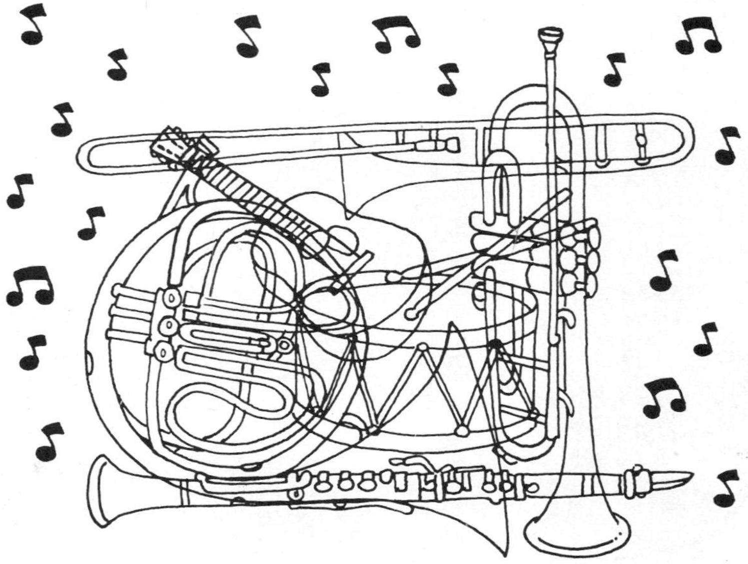

ANSWER: THERE ARE SIX MUSICAL INSTRUMENTS.